Delaware Wetlands:

Status and Changes from 1992 to 2007

Acknowledgments

This booklet reflects the work of the U.S. Fish and Wildlife Service (FWS), the Delaware Department of Natural Resources and Environmental Control (DNREC), and Virginia Polytechnic Institute and State University (Virginia Tech). Most of the information comes from an update of wetland inventory data produced by the FWS's National Wetlands Inventory Program (NWI) and DNREC. Principal investigator for the work in Sussex County was Ralph Tiner (FWS), while Mark Biddle (DNREC) and Amy Jacobs (DNREC) were co-principal investigators for similar work in Kent and New Castle Counties. The data in this report were derived through on-screen image analysis and geographic information system (GIS) analysis techniques by Kevin McGuckin and personnel at Virginia Tech's Conservation Management Institute: Nicole Fuhrman, Matthew Fields, Pamela Swint, Jason Herman, David Orndorff, and Steven Quagliata. Alison Rogerson (DNREC), Rebecca Rothweiler (DNREC), and Kristin Berry (University of Delaware) provided graphics for the report. We also thank people who contributed photographs for use in this publication. Photo credits are shown for each photo. Layout and Graphic Design: Jennie Hess, State of Delaware Printing and Publishing Office. Funding was provided by EPA grant CD-97368601-0 and the U.S. Fish and Wildlife Service.

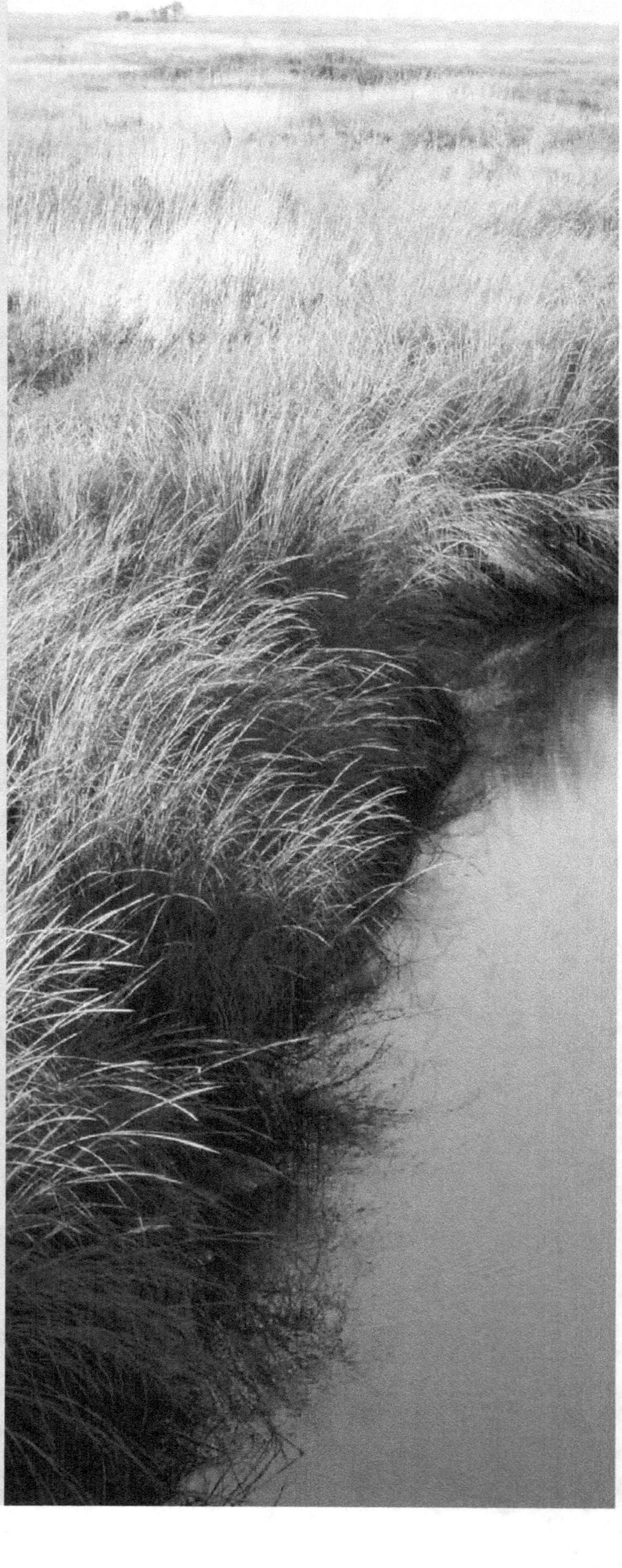

This report should be cited as follows:

Tiner, R.W., M.A. Biddle, A.D. Jacobs, A.B. Rogerson and K.G. McGuckin. 2011. *Delaware Wetlands: Status and Changes from 1992 to 2007.* Cooperative National Wetlands Inventory Publication. U.S. Fish and Wildlife Service, Northeast Region, Hadley, MA and the Delaware Department of Natural Resources and Environmental Control, Dover, DE. 35 pp.

Delaware Wetlands:
Status and Changes from 1992 to 2007

Ralph W. Tiner[1], Mark A. Biddle[2], Amy D. Jacobs[2], Alison B. Rogerson[2] and Kevin G. McGuckin[3]

A Cooperative National Wetlands Inventory Publication with funding support from the Delaware Department of Natural Resources and Environmental Control and the U.S. Environmental Protection Agency.

September 2011
Copies of this booklet may be obtained online at:
www.dnrec.delaware.gov/Admin/DelawareWetlands or
http://www.fws.gov/northeast/wetlands/

Contents

Cover photo: Cherry Walk fen (classifications: palustrine emergent wetland seasonally flooded and terrene basin outflow-estuarine discharge wetland; *Robert Coxe, Delaware Natural Heritage and Endangered Species Program*)

Cover photo insets: mud turtle (*Kinosternon subrubrum*), elongated lobelia (Lobelia elongata), elfin skimmer (*Nannothemis bella*), purple pitcher-plant (*Sarracenia purpurea*); *DNHESP and Chris Bennett Delaware State Parks Environmental Stewardship Program*

Photo Left: an estuarine emergent wetland irregularly flooded and estuarine fringe bidirectional-tidal wetland; *Anthony Jackson, DNHESP*

Back Cover photo: a palustrine emergent wetland semi-permanently flooded and terrene fringe throughflow; *Anthony Jackson, DNHESP*

[1] Regional Wetland Coordinator, U.S. Fish and Wildlife Service, Ecological Services, National Wetlands Inventory Program, 300 Westgate Center Drive, Hadley, MA 01035

[2] Delaware Department of Natural Resources, Watershed Assessment Section, Division of Watershed Stewardship, 820 Silver Lake Boulevard, Suite 220, Dover, DE 19904

[3] Conservation Management Institute, 1900 Kraft Drive, Blacksburg, VA 24060-6145

Sunrise over tidal marsh (classifications: estuarine emergent wetland regularly flooded and estuarine fringe bidirectional-tidal wetland; *Anthony Jackson, DNHESP*)

Executive Summary

As much as 25 percent of Delaware is covered by a variety of wetland types, from coastal salt marshes to rare Delmarva Bays. Wetlands provide important benefits to people and the environment by improving water quality, reducing flooding and erosion, providing habitat for plants and animals, decreasing the impact of severe storms, and providing recreational opportunities.

Changes in wetlands result from both human activities and natural processes such as droughts, rising sea level, hurricanes, episodic floods, fire and animal activity. The most common human impacts that eliminate or degrade wetlands include filling, draining, dredging, conversion to other uses, pond construction, channelization, discharging pollutants and the spread of invasive plants.

A previous inventory and assessment of wetland changes for the state were completed for 1981-1992 and summarized in "Delaware Wetlands: Status and Recent Trends" (Tiner 2001). The current mapping and analysis effort is largely an update of that study and was completed by the U.S. Fish and Wildlife Service's National Wetlands Inventory Program (NWI) and Delaware's Department of Natural Resources and Environmental Control (DNREC). This report summarizes the 2007 status of wetlands across Delaware, details findings from the trends analysis of how and where wetlands were gained or lost between 1992 and 2007, and provides perspective on how those changes affect wetland functions and the future of Delaware wetlands.

Wetlands in this inventory were classified in two ways: by major ecological types and abiotic properties. Ecological types use biological, physical and chemical characteristics whereas abiotic properties address position on the landscape, landform, and direction of water flow. This mapping effort mapped 320,076 acres of wetlands across the state of Delaware. This total includes 62,291 acres of hydric soil map units that were naturally vegetated but did not exhibit a distinctive wet signature on the aerial imagery. These areas are likely to support seasonally saturated wetlands which are among the most difficult wetlands to identify.

Delaware's wetlands are dominated by palustrine forests which make up 64 percent of the state's wetlands. Estuarine emergent wetlands comprise 23 percent of the wetlands statewide. Forty-seven percent of Delaware's wetlands are located in Sussex County, 38 percent in Kent and 15 percent in New Castle County. Forty-two percent of Delaware's wetlands fall within the Delaware Bay Basin, 42 percent in the Chesapeake Basin, 14 percent in the Inland Bays Basin, and two percent in the Piedmont Basin.

We used a landscape-scale assessment based on NWIPlus classifications to predict the ability of the state's wetlands to potentially perform 11 wetland functions. Nearly two-thirds or more of the state's wetlands have the potential to perform the following functions at high or moderate levels: surface water detention, nutrient transformation, carbon sequestration, bank and shoreline stabilization, and provision of habitat for other wildlife. Other functions predicted to be provided by more than 40 percent of the state's wetlands are streamflow maintenance, sediment retention, and provision of habitat for waterfowl, waterbirds, fish and shellfish. About one-third of the wetlands are important for coastal storm surge detention and about one-fifth have the potential to serve well as vital habitat for unique, uncommon or highly diverse plant communities.

Wetland changes were determined by comparing aerial images from 1992 and 2007. This evaluation indicated that nearly 3,900 acres of vegetated wetlands were lost through conversion to another land use, while 768 acres of vegetated wetlands were created or restored. These changes resulted in a net loss of 3,126 acres of vegetated wetlands statewide. Palustrine vegetated wetlands were lost due to conversion to agriculture (33%), development (30%), extraction/transition (28%), pond and lake construction (4%) and highway and roads (2%). Most of the net palustrine loss was forested wetlands (2,931 acres). Estuarine vegetated wetlands had a net loss of 238 acres between 1992 and 2007. Causes for the estuarine vegetated

wetlands loss were conversion to estuarine open water (83%), intertidal shores (10%), development (4%), beach overwash (2%), and pond construction (1%).

While losing vegetated wetlands, Delaware experienced a net gain of 2,285 acres of ponds and tidal mudflats over the 15-year study period. About two-thirds (65%) of the new pond acreage was built on former agricultural land for use as stormwater ponds for new residential and commercial developments. Another three percent were created on already developed lands and ten percent were constructed in extraction/transition areas, often in borrow pits. Seven percent of ponds were created in or from existing wetlands, and 15 percent were built in upland forests or fallow fields.

Changes in Delaware's wetlands between 1992 and 2007 have increased nonvegetated wetland types (mainly ponds) that perform limited wetland functions while vegetated wetlands decreased or became debilitated, thereby reducing their ability to provide most functions. The newly created nonvegetated wetlands do not, however, compensate for the heavy losses of vegetated wetlands because they provide less functions and services than vegetated wetlands. During the 15-year study period, most wetland functions experienced a decline.

Despite improved public-private sector collaboration, increased research and successful restoration efforts, Delaware's wetlands faced a myriad of challenges during the 15 years examined by this study. Recent U.S. Supreme Court decisions have weakened wetland jurisdiction, while the real estate boom intensified pressure for development and infrastructure construction. In addition to direct impacts, this often produced secondary impacts to wetlands, increased flooding, and degraded water quality.

The state's annual vegetated wetland loss rate increased nine percent compared to a similar study for 1981/2-1992. State tidal wetland regulations have helped curb the loss of estuarine wetlands, yet freshwater vegetated wetlands experienced heavy losses from 1992 to 2007. Watershed wetland-health studies across the state have found that the majority of the remaining wetlands have been degraded to varying extents. Climate change, especially rising sea levels will produce increased threats to wetlands in the future. Without strengthened freshwater wetland regulations and improved permit tracking and enforcement, Delaware will likely continue to suffer the loss and degradation of its wetland resources and the valuable environmental services they provide.

Introduction

Wetlands represent the collection of marshes, swamps, bogs, wet meadows, wet flatwoods, and other seasonally waterlogged environments that occur across the landscape. They are lands that are periodically flooded or saturated near the surface for periods long enough to affect plant growth and soil development. Scientists have determined that the minimum wetness for a wetland is saturation within one foot of the ground surface for two weeks or more during the growing season in most years (every other year on average)[2], yet wetlands are also wet for much of the non-growing season (from late fall to early spring). These conditions create waterlogged soils (hydric soils) and substrates that are essentially devoid of oxygen for significant periods. Plants colonizing such sites are called "hydrophytes" (water-loving plants) because they possess special adaptations that allow them to grow and reproduce in oxygen-deficient (anaerobic) saturated and/or flooded soils. Hydric soils exhibit unique characteristics reflective of prolonged and frequent anaerobic conditions. Consequently, the presence of hydrophytic vegetation, hydric soils, and hydrology (flooding or soil saturation) are used as indicators of wetlands and for delineating their boundaries.

Examples of organic soils (left) and mineral soils (right) with thick dark surfaces overlying greyish subsoils are typical hydric soils in Delaware. (DNREC Wetland Monitoring and Assessment Program)

[2] Source: Wetlands Characteristics and Boundaries (1995) published by National Academy Press, Washington, DC 20418.

Atlantic White Cedar swamp (classifications: palustrine forested wetland seasonally flooded and saturated and lotic stream basin throughflow wetland; *DNREC WMAP*)

Wetlands have formed along the shores of the Delaware and Inland Bays, various rivers and streams, in depressions or basins (including ponds and impoundments), on broad flat areas between stream systems (interfluves) and in the headwater regions of streams. These are places subjected to frequent flooding or prolonged saturation associated with seasonal high water tables. Wetlands receive water from precipitation, surface water runoff, groundwater discharge, and tides. Some are flooded year-round, daily or periodically by tides or river overflow (e.g., tidal marshes and floodplain wetlands), while others are never inundated but have water tables at or near the surface for a few months (e.g., wet flatwoods or winter wet woods). The latter are among the most difficult wetlands for the average person to recognize due to the lack of standing surface water. A full list of wetland types and descriptions can be found online http://www.dnrec.delaware.gov/Admin/DelawareWetlands/Pages/default.aspx

This report summarizes the findings of the recent wetland inventory and trends analysis performed by the NWI and DNREC and gives readers perspective on the current status of the state's wetlands, how they changed from 1992-2007, the significance of those changes from a wetland function standpoint, and the future of Delaware's wetlands. It also provides a list of resource agencies and additional sources where readers can obtain more information about the state's wetlands and wetlands in general.

Wetland Functions and Values

Wetlands provide many benefits and services to people, wildlife, and the environment every day. They reduce flooding by absorbing runoff, clean our water by removing sediments and pollutants, decrease the impact of severe storms, stabilize shorelines, provide habitat for plants and animals including rare and endangered species, and offer educational and recreational opportunities. While individual wetlands provide these functions, their contribution to an entire watershed or the state is enhanced by a whole network of wetlands working together to provide environmental services (Figure 1). When wetlands are removed from the landscape or degraded, replacement of the services they would normally supply can cost significant amounts of time and money.

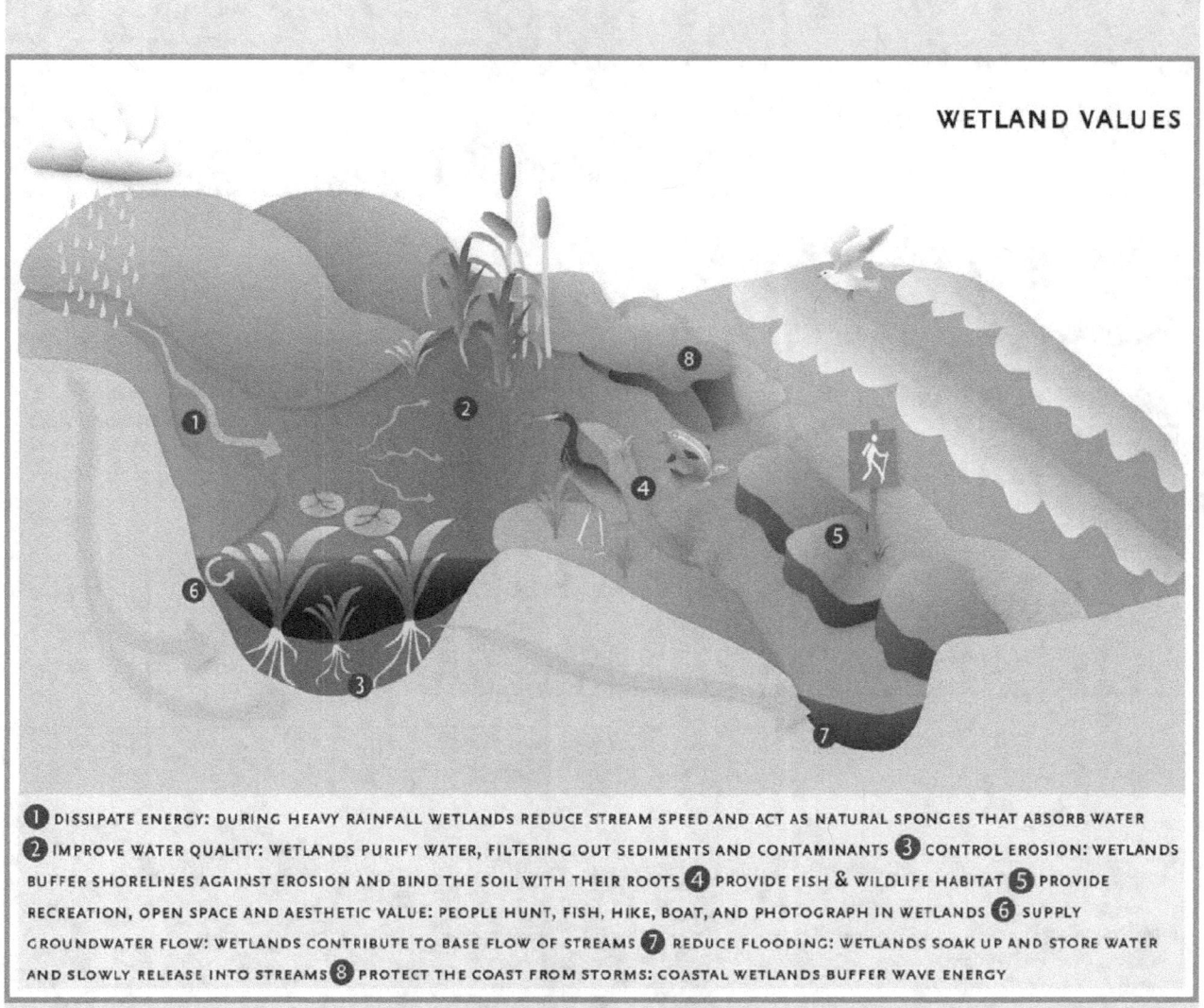

WETLAND VALUES

① DISSIPATE ENERGY: DURING HEAVY RAINFALL WETLANDS REDUCE STREAM SPEED AND ACT AS NATURAL SPONGES THAT ABSORB WATER ② IMPROVE WATER QUALITY: WETLANDS PURIFY WATER, FILTERING OUT SEDIMENTS AND CONTAMINANTS ③ CONTROL EROSION: WETLANDS BUFFER SHORELINES AGAINST EROSION AND BIND THE SOIL WITH THEIR ROOTS ④ PROVIDE FISH & WILDLIFE HABITAT ⑤ PROVIDE RECREATION, OPEN SPACE AND AESTHETIC VALUE: PEOPLE HUNT, FISH, HIKE, BOAT, AND PHOTOGRAPH IN WETLANDS ⑥ SUPPLY GROUNDWATER FLOW: WETLANDS CONTRIBUTE TO BASE FLOW OF STREAMS ⑦ REDUCE FLOODING: WETLANDS SOAK UP AND STORE WATER AND SLOWLY RELEASE INTO STREAMS ⑧ PROTECT THE COAST FROM STORMS: COASTAL WETLANDS BUFFER WAVE ENERGY

Figure 1. Wetlands provide many functions and services that make them among the world's most valuable natural resources.

Wetland Classification

Wetlands can be grouped in various ways based on vegetation, landscape position, function, disturbance, and other properties. For purposes of this wetland inventory and change analysis, wetlands are classified in two ways: 1) ecological properties (vegetation, water regime, and salinity) and 2) abiotic properties (landscape position, landform, and water flow path). Ecological classification has been reported in the previous Delaware Status and Trends report, but the addition of abiotic characteristics allows

Salt marsh along the Murderkill River (classifications: estuarine emergent wetland regularly flooded and estuarine fringe bidirectional-tidal wetland; *DNREC WMAP*)

Floodplain swamp at White Clay Creek State Park (classifications: palustrine forested wetland temporarily flooded and lotic stream flat throughflow wetland; *Robert Coxe, DNHESP*)

Maple-alder swamp at Prime Hook NWR (classifications: palustrine scrub-shrub wetland seasonally flooded-tidal and lotic river floodplain bidirectional-tidal wetland; *Robert Coxe, DNHESP*)

more inference on the potential of wetlands to perform functions. For descriptions of the plant communities growing in Delaware wetlands, see *Wetlands of Delaware*

(http://www.fws.gov/wetlands/_documents/g0ther/WetlandsOfDelaware.pdf)

WETLANDS CLASSIFIED BY ECOLOGICAL PROPERTIES

According to the U.S. Fish and Wildlife Service's wetland classification system, wetlands occur in five ecological systems: 1) marine (open ocean and associated shoreline), 2) estuarine (estuary where fresh water mixes with sea water through tidal action), 3) riverine (rivers and their shorelines), 4) lacustrine (lakes, reservoirs, and their shorelines), and 5) palustrine (freshwater floodplain, headwater, and isolated wetlands including ponds) (Figure 2). The majority of Delaware wetlands fall into two systems: estuarine and palustrine. These wetlands include both vegetated and nonvegetated types. Estuarine wetlands are intertidal salt to brackish environments including vegetated wetlands such as tidal marshes and nonvegetated wetlands like mudflats and sandy beaches associated with coastal embayments and brackish rivers and streams. They have salinities ranging from above sea strength (hyperhaline >40 parts per thousand [ppt]) to slightly brackish (1 to 5 ppt), with the latter subject to fresh water conditions during spring runoff. Palustrine wetlands are freshwater, waterlogged or flooded habitats. They are mostly vegetated habitats like marshes, wet meadows, swamps, and wet flatwoods (winter wet woods), yet also include nonvegetated types mainly shallow ponds. While most palustrine wetlands are nontidal, freshwater tidal wetlands are also part of this group. Less common wetland types in Delaware are marine wetlands (limited to the shore of the Atlantic Ocean; sea beaches), riverine wetlands (within river channels and most abundant in the daily intertidal zone of rivers where they transition from tidal to nontidal), and lacustrine wetlands (the shallow water zone of lakes, reservoirs, and large impoundments).

WETLANDS CLASSIFIED BY ABIOTIC PROPERTIES

Wetlands can also be described by features including their position on the landscape, landform, and the directional flow of water. These abiotic properties (also called hydrogeomorphic features), when

Figure 2. The same wetland can be classified in terms of ecological properties (Cowardin et al. 1979; *pg7*) or by abiotic factors (LLWW descriptors: Tiner 2003; *pg8*).

Original art by John Norton reinterpreted by Kristin Berry

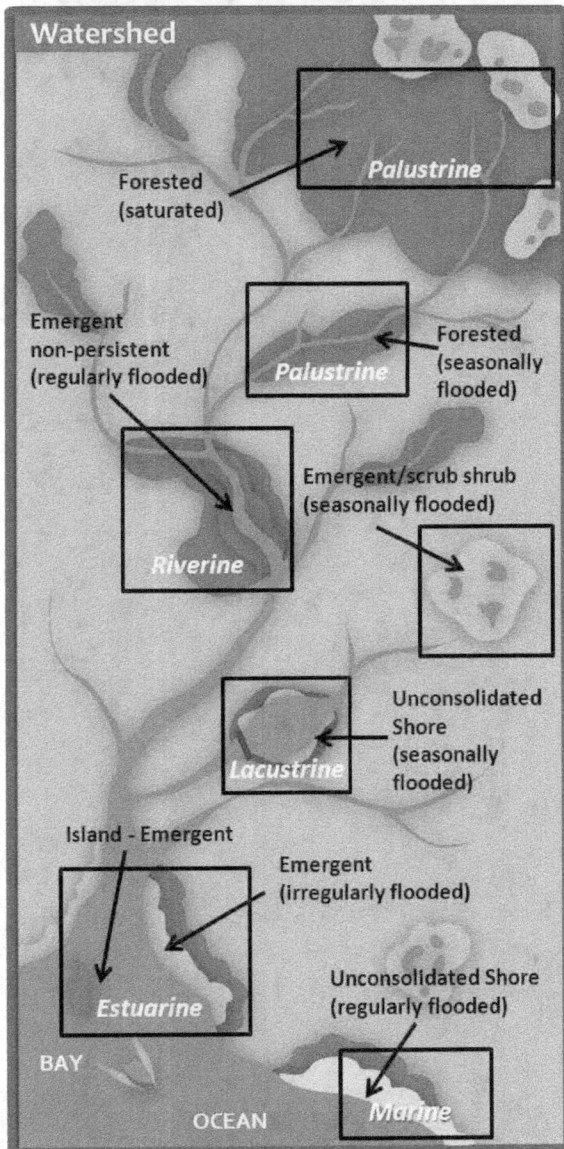

Wetlands Described by Ecological Properties

Watershed

Forested (saturated)

Palustrine

Emergent non-persistent (regularly flooded)

Palustrine

Forested (seasonally flooded)

Emergent/scrub shrub (seasonally flooded)

Riverine

Unconsolidated Shore (seasonally flooded)

Lacustrine

Island - Emergent

Emergent (irregularly flooded)

Estuarine

Unconsolidated Shore (regularly flooded)

BAY

OCEAN

Marine

Key: System - white italicized, Class vegetation/substrate – text from arrow, Water regime - in parenthesis

Palustrine - floodplain, headwater, and isolated wetlands including ponds
Riverine - rivers, streams, and their shorelines
Lacustrine - lakes reservoirs, and their shorelines
Estuarine - estuary where fresh water mixes with sea water through tidal action
Marine - open ocean and associated shoreline
*These are examples only.

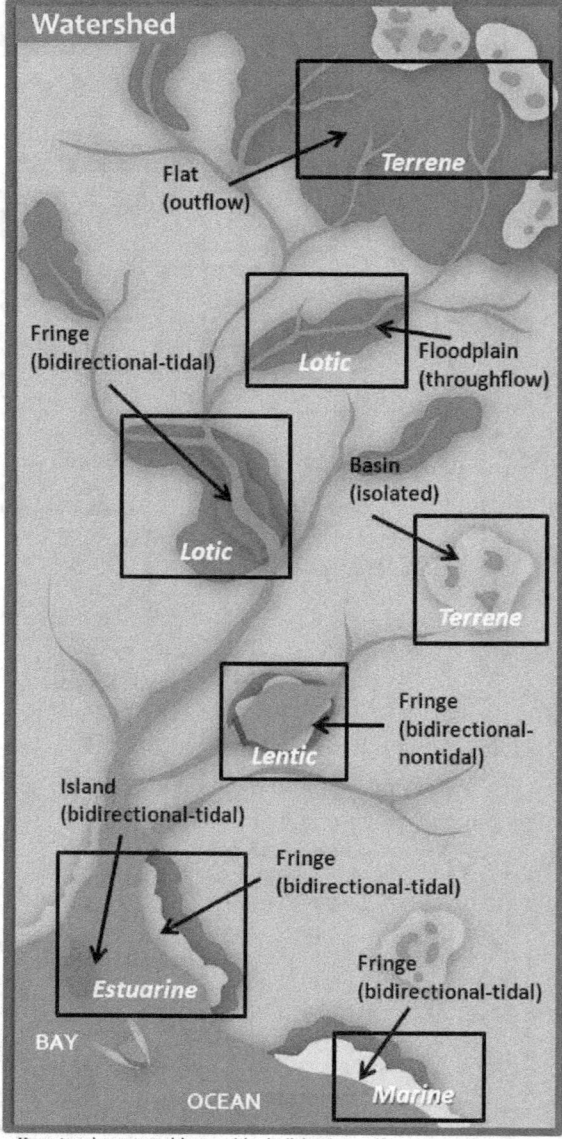

Wetlands Described by Abiotic Factors

Watershed

Flat
(outflow)

Terrene

Fringe
(bidirectional-tidal)

Lotic

Floodplain
(throughflow)

Basin
(isolated)

Lotic

Terrene

Fringe
(bidirectional-nontidal)

Lentic

Island
(bidirectional-tidal)

Fringe
(bidirectional-tidal)

Fringe
(bidirectional-tidal)

Estuarine

BAY

Marine

OCEAN

Key: Landscape position - white italicized, Landform - text from arrow, Water flow path - in parenthesis

Terrene - floodplain, headwater, and isolated wetlands including ponds
Lotic - rivers and streams
Lentic - in basins of lakes and reservoirs
Estuarine - along tidal brackish waters
Marine - along the ocean
*These are examples only.

added to the U.S. Fish and Wildlife Service wetland types, produce a more detailed characterization of wetland types across the landscape and generate information that can be used to predict wetland functions.

Wetlands can be placed in five landscape positions which relate to their location relative to a waterbody, if present: 1) marine (along the ocean), 2) estuarine (along tidal brackish waters), 3) lotic (on floodplains of rivers and streams), 4) lentic (within basins of lakes, reservoirs, and impoundments ≥ 20 acres), and 5) terrene (in headwaters and interfluves generally surrounded by uplands) (Figure 2). The first two positions are equivalent to the marine and estuarine ecological systems, so the landscape position descriptor is best for separating various types of freshwater wetlands into other categories based on their association with a river, stream, lake, or pond, or by their lack of a connection to surface water.

Landform describes the physical shape of the wetland with several types recognized: basin (depressional wetland including those along streams), flat (wetland on a nearly level plain), floodplain (overflow land along rivers and subject to periodic inundation), fringe (wetland in water or within the banks of a river), island (wetland completely surrounded by water), and slope (wetland on a hillside).

Water flow path defines the directional flow of water associated with a wetland. If the wetland is the source of a stream or seep, it is an outflow wetland. River and streamside wetlands are throughflow wetlands with water running through them (both into and out of) during high water periods. Wetlands that only receive water from channelized flow without any outflow are considered inflow wetlands; there are few, if any, of this type in Delaware. Some wetlands have no channelized inflow or outflow – they are isolated, essentially with no water flow path, although water is exchanged via precipitation, evapotranspiration, runoff from the land and groundwater recharge and discharge. Wetlands along lakes and reservoirs have water levels that rise and fall with lake levels - bidirectional-nontidal. Tidal wetlands experience bidirectional-tidal flow with ebb and flood tides. Water flow path as applied in this inventory typically emphasizes directional flow of surface water and while groundwater/subsurface flows occur (Figure 3), they require detailed hydrologic studies that were beyond the scope of this inventory. For more information on the abiotic descriptors go to
http://library.fws.gov/Wetlands/dichotomouskeys0903.pdf

A. POORLY DRAINED UPLAND, WELL DRAINED UPLAND, AND COASTAL WETLAND AND BEACH

WESTERN DELAWARE ──────► EASTERN DELAWARE

POORLY DRAINED UPLAND   WELL DRAINED UPLAND

PALUSTRINE WETLAND   PALUSTRINE WETLANDS   PAL USTRINE WETLANDS

COASTAL WETLAND AND BEACH

HEADWATER FOREST   ISOLATED DEPRESSION   ISOLATED DEPRESSION   STREAM   STREAM

ESTUARINE WETLAND   ESTUARINE WETLANDS

TIDAL STREAM   ESTUARY

SAND AQUIFER

CONFINING UNIT

SALTWATER

FRESHWATER   ESTUARINE DEPOSITS

B. SURFICIAL CONFINED REGION

UPSTREAM ──────► DOWNSTREAM

PALUSTRINE WETLANDS   PALUSTRINE WETLANDS

RIVERINE WETLAND   RIVERINE WETLAND   RIVERINE WETLAND

DITCH   STREAM   RIVER

SAND AQUIFER (UPPER UNIT)

SAND AQUIFER (UPPER UNIT)

CONFINING UNIT   CONFINING UNIT

SAND AQUIFER (LOWER UNIT)

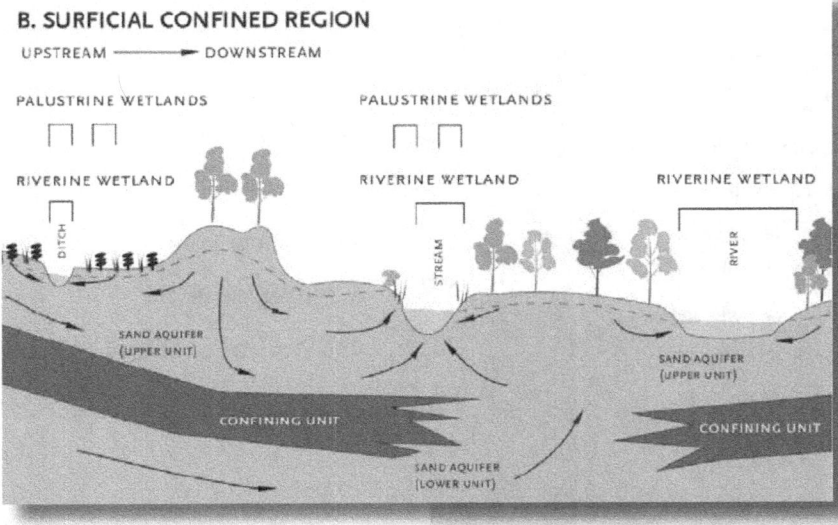

Figure 3. Regional depiction of Delaware's wetland types showing groundwater flow paths that create wetlands.

Flow path varies laterally across the state (A), from upstream to downstream (B), and longitudinally along the state (C). Wetlands form where groundwater discharges, surface water accumulates, or in low areas subject to tidal flooding or river overflows.

(Adapted from M. A. Hayes. 1996. Delaware wetland resources. In: National Water Summary on Wetland Resources. U.S. Geological Survey, Reston, VA. Water-Supply Paper 2425. pp.147-152)

C. PIEDMONT PROVINCE AND INNER COASTAL PLAIN

NORTHERN DELAWARE ──────► SOUTHERN DELAWARE

PIEDMONT PROVINCE   INNER COASTAL PLAIN

RIVERINE WETLANDS

PALUSTRINE WETLAND

PALUSTRINE WETLANDS   ESTUARINE WETLAND

STREAM   POND   CHESAPEAKE AND DELAWARE CANAL

RIVERINE WETLANDS

STREAM   STREAM

SAND AQUIFER

FRACTURED BEDROCK   CONFINING UNIT

SAND AQUIFER

Methods for Determining Wetland Status and Trends

This report is based on an update of wetland inventory data by the U.S. Fish and Wildlife Service's National Wetlands Inventory (NWI) Program and the Delaware Department of Natural Resources and Environmental Control (DNREC). The inventory generated updated information on wetland status (2007), changes from 1992 to 2007, and provided an assessment of the potential of wetlands to perform certain functions based on wetland classification. The study involved interpreting wetlands on aerial imagery and comparing changes by examining aerial photographs from 1992 and 2007 (McGuckin 2011).

Wetlands were classified and mapped according to the Federal Geographic Data Committee's wetland classification and mapping standards (FGDC 2009). 'H-wetlands' were identified by consulting USDA soils survey data and aerial imagery. They represent hydric soil map units that supported natural vegetation but lacked a photointerpretable 'wet signature' - undeveloped hydric soil areas that likely contain at least some wetland. More detailed wetland classification included abiotic properties for landscape position, landform, water flow path and water body type (LLWW descriptors; Tiner 2003) to create an expanded wetland database for predicting wetland functions at the landscape level.

Wetland changes were identified as losses, gains, or changes in type with the nature of the change in land or land cover type specified. Losses were identified as areas mapped in 1992 that were converted to nonwetlands or deepwater habitats by 2007. Gains were identified as mapped wetland in 2007 that were not present in 1992. Major causes of wetland change were attributed to: 1) industrial development, 2) commercial development, 3) residential development, 4) highways and roads, 5) ponds, 6) transitional land (land undergoing some type of development - unknown use), 7) rangeland (open fields and thickets), 8) cropland, 9) pasture, and 10) upland forest. Wetlands also changed from one wetland type to another by human-induced actions, mainly timber harvest, pond

creation, and extraction operations. Changes as small as 0.1 acre were identified.

Statewide trends were analyzed and compiled for all three counties and the state's four major drainage basins: 1) Piedmont, 2) Delaware Bay, 3) Chesapeake Bay, and 4) Inland Bays (Figure 4). Wetland status and trends by wetland type are reported statewide, by county and by drainage basin.

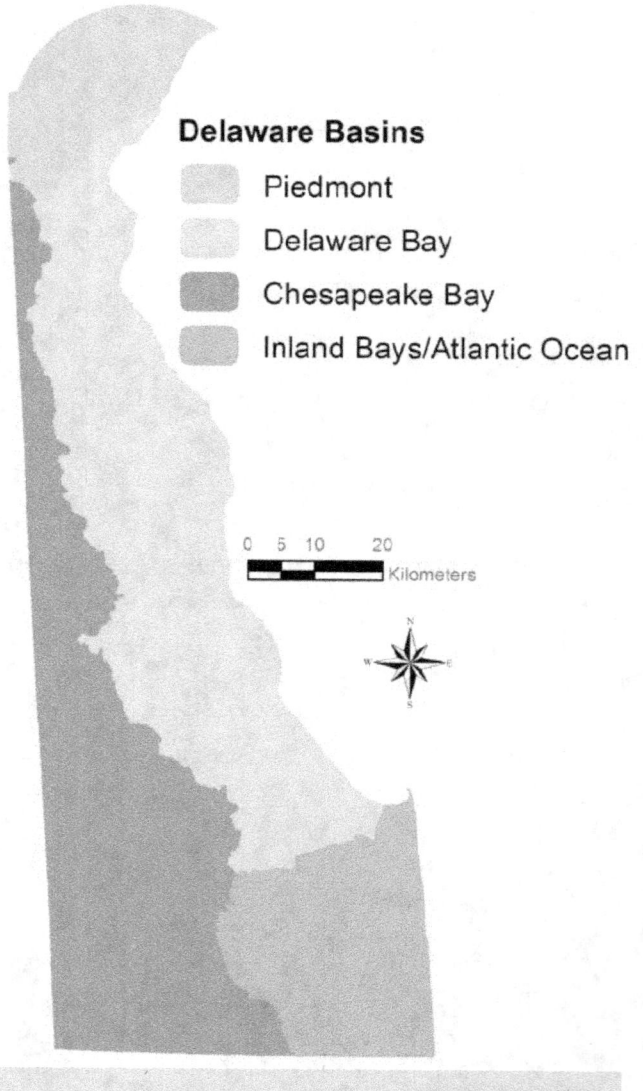

Delaware Basins

Piedmont
Delaware Bay
Chesapeake Bay
Inland Bays/Atlantic Ocean

0 5 10   20
Kilometers

Figure 4. Drainage basins in Delaware.

Wetland acreages based on remote sensing often produce different results. This is especially true given differences in image quality and scale. The previous 1992 wetland inventory utilized 1:12,000 color infrared aerial photography, whereas the current survey used 1-foot resolution true color digital imagery. Mapping tends to be more generalized at smaller scales. The 1992 survey produced a statewide wetland estimate of 353,878 acres derived from an examination of wetlands for 60 percent of the state (Tiner 2001). This figure is over 30,000 acres more than what is now reported based on a complete statewide inventory. The higher totals from the earlier inventory resulted from several factors related to differences in survey methods, interpretations, and computations. The differences include: 1) estimating wetland acreage for 40 percent of the state that was not examined, 2) treatment of farmed wetlands, 3) computation of estuarine wetland acreage, and 4) tabulations of lacustrine and riverine wetlands and waters. The previous work identified 29,215 acres of farmed wetlands while the present survey reported only 679 acres (this difference in farmed wetlands was not factored into current loss). The present survey treated most of the previously mapped farmed wetlands as potential wetland restoration sites since their hydrology has been severely altered to the point that they are not likely to perform wetland functions in a significant way. The difference in estuarine vegetated wetland acreage appears due to a computational error as the total is greater than what is currently found in the DNREC database (nearly 74,000 acres). The 1992 total inadvertently included lacustrine and riverine deepwater habitats in the wetland acreage. The statewide wetland acreage determined by the current survey is 320,076 acres including 62,291 acres of "H-wetlands" defined as hydric soil map units exhibiting natural vegetation but lacking a photointerpretable wet signature. Proportions of individual wetland types by region or county compared to state totals are all based on the state total of 320,076 acres.

A coastal plain pond located in the Blackbird watershed (classifications: palustrine forested/scrub-shrub wetland seasonally flooded and terrene basin outflow wetland; *DNREC WMAP*).

Current Status of Wetlands

WETLAND STATUS BY ECOLOGICAL PROPERTIES

Twenty-five percent of the state is covered by wetlands, with 320,076 acres inventoried (Table 1; see accompanying Map 1 for general distribution of types). Palustrine wetlands are the predominant wetland type comprising roughly 76 percent of the state's wetlands. Estuarine wetlands make up the bulk of the remaining wetlands at more than 23%, with only a few lacustrine, marine, and riverine wetlands recorded (each <1%; Figure 5). More than 85 percent of Delaware's palustrine wetlands are forested, while seven percent are scrub-shrub types and about four percent are emergent types. Salt marshes are the dominant emergent type of estuarine wetlands representing 96 percent of this type. A total of 667 acres along the ocean shoreline represent the state's marine wetlands. Other wetlands such as ponds (unconsolidated bottom) and farmed wetlands comprise the rest of the wetlands.

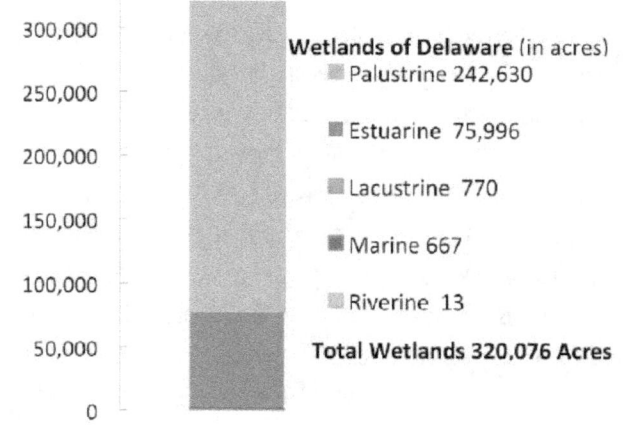

Wetlands of Delaware (in acres)
- Palustrine 242,630
- Estuarine 75,996
- Lacustrine 770
- Marine 667
- Riverine 13

Total Wetlands 320,076 Acres

Figure 5. Composition of Delaware wetlands by acreage.

A beaver swamp in the St. Jones River watershed (classifications: palustrine emergent/ forested wetland seasonally flooded and lotic stream basin throughflow wetland; *DNREC WMAP*).

Table 1. 2007 acreage of wetlands classified by ecological characteristics for Delaware. Totals include H-wetlands (hydric soil areas with natural vegetation but lacking a photo interpretable wet signature).

Note: Acreage in parentheses is the acreage of palustrine freshwater tidal wetlands mapped in that class.

System	Subsystem		Class	Acreage (*tidal only acreage*)
Marine	Intertidal		Unconsolidated Shore	667
	Total Marine			667
Estuarine	Intertidal			
		Vegetated	Scrub-Shrub	705
			Emergent	72,839
			Forested	153
			Aquatic Bed	645
			Total Vegetated	*74,342*
		Nonvegetated		
			Unconsolidated Shore	1,654
	Total Estuarine			75,996
Palustrine		Vegetated		
			Emergent	10,938 (1,250)
			Forested	206,254 (6,150)
			Scrub-Shrub	18,434 (2,683)
			Farmed	679
			Total Vegetated	*236,305* (10,083)
		Nonvegetated		
			Aquatic Bed	131 (12)
			Unconsolidated Bottom	6,117 (145)
			Unconsolidated Shore	77 (46)
			Total Nonvegetated	*6,325* (203)
	Total Palustrine			242,630 (10,286)
Lacustrine	Littoral		Emergent	1
			Unconsolidated Bottom	769
	Total Lacustrine			770
Riverine	Tidal		Unconsolidated Shore	11
	Lower Perennial		Unconsolidated Shore	2
	Total Riverine			13
TOTAL MAPPED				320,076

Eighty-four percent of the state's wetlands were found in two basins: the Delaware Bay Basin and the Chesapeake Bay Basin in nearly equal amounts (Figure 6). Fourteen percent were in the Inland Bays Basin, and two percent in the Piedmont Basin. Estuarine emergent wetlands were the predominant wetland type in the Delaware Bay Basin and palustrine forested wetlands dominated the rest of the basins.

About 47 percent of the state's wetlands were in Sussex County, 38 percent in Kent County, and 15 percent in New Castle County (Figure 7). Palustrine wetlands were nearly two and four times more abundant than estuarine wetlands in Kent and Sussex Counties, respectively, while more equal amounts were found in New Castle County. Marine wetlands only occurred in Sussex County, whereas lacustrine wetlands (adjacent to mill ponds) were most abundant in Kent County.

Ninety-six percent of the state's estuarine wetlands were emergent wetlands, and two percent were unconsolidated shores (beach or mud flat) (Figure 8). Scrub-shrub, aquatic beds and forested types made up <1% each. Palustrine wetlands were dominated by forested wetlands, representing 85 percent of the acreage. Scrub-shrub types made up over seven percent of palustrine wetlands, emergent accounted for over four percent and ponds over two percent. Farmed wetlands, aquatic beds and shores made up <1% each (Figure 8).

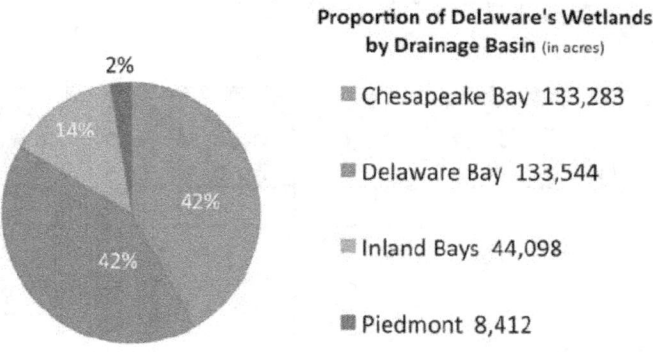

Proportion of Delaware's Wetlands by Drainage Basin (in acres)

- Chesapeake Bay 133,283
- Delaware Bay 133,544
- Inland Bays 44,098
- Piedmont 8,412

Figure 6. Acreage of wetlands by drainage basin in Delaware. These totals exclude marine wetlands.

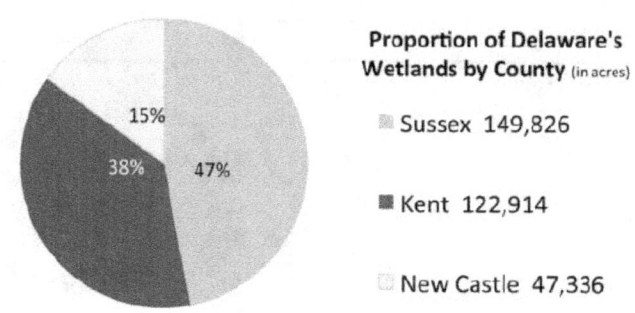

Proportion of Delaware's Wetlands by County (in acres)

- Sussex 149,826
- Kent 122,914
- New Castle 47,336

Figure 7. Delaware wetland acreage by county.

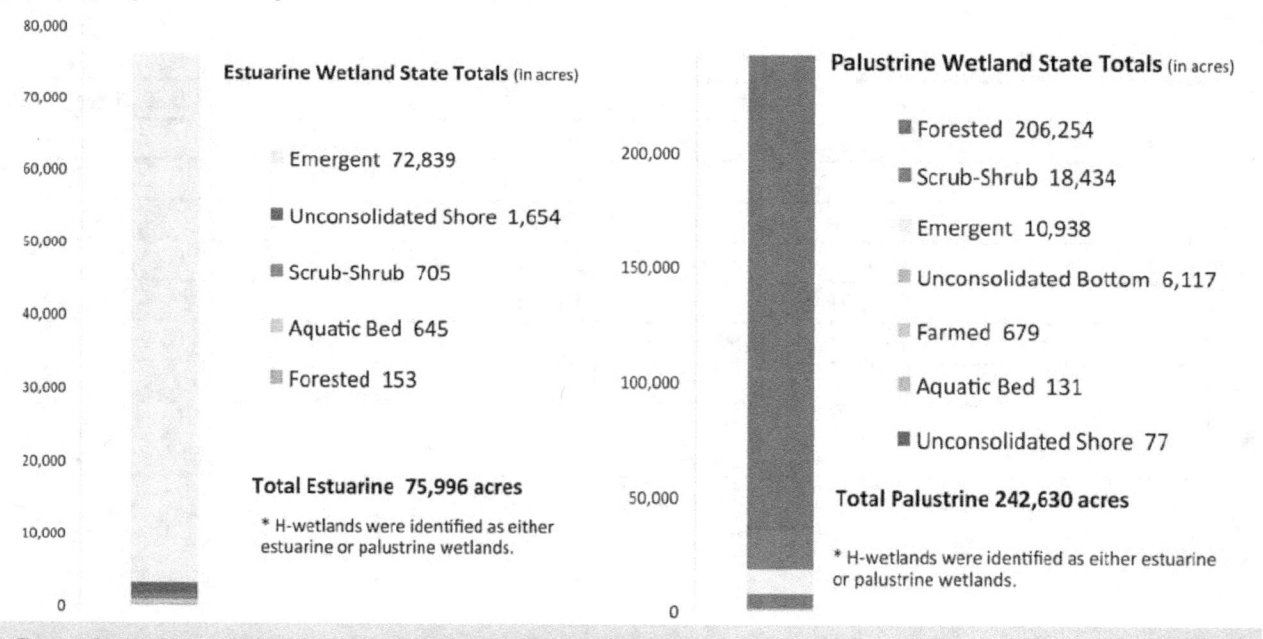

Estuarine Wetland State Totals (in acres)

- Emergent 72,839
- Unconsolidated Shore 1,654
- Scrub-Shrub 705
- Aquatic Bed 645
- Forested 153

Total Estuarine 75,996 acres

* H-wetlands were identified as either estuarine or palustrine wetlands.

Palustrine Wetland State Totals (in acres)

- Forested 206,254
- Scrub-Shrub 18,434
- Emergent 10,938
- Unconsolidated Bottom 6,117
- Farmed 679
- Aquatic Bed 131
- Unconsolidated Shore 77

Total Palustrine 242,630 acres

* H-wetlands were identified as either estuarine or palustrine wetlands.

Figure 8. Statewide acreage of estuarine (left) and palustrine (right) wetland types in Delaware.

2007 Delaware Wetlands

Shown by Landsape Position (Ecological System)

 Lotic River (Palustrine)

 Lotic Stream (Palustrine)

 Terrene Basin (Palustrine)

 Terrene Flat (Palustrine)

 Marine (Marine)

Open Salt Water

Estuarine (Estuarine)

 Lentic (Palustrine)

 H-wetlands*

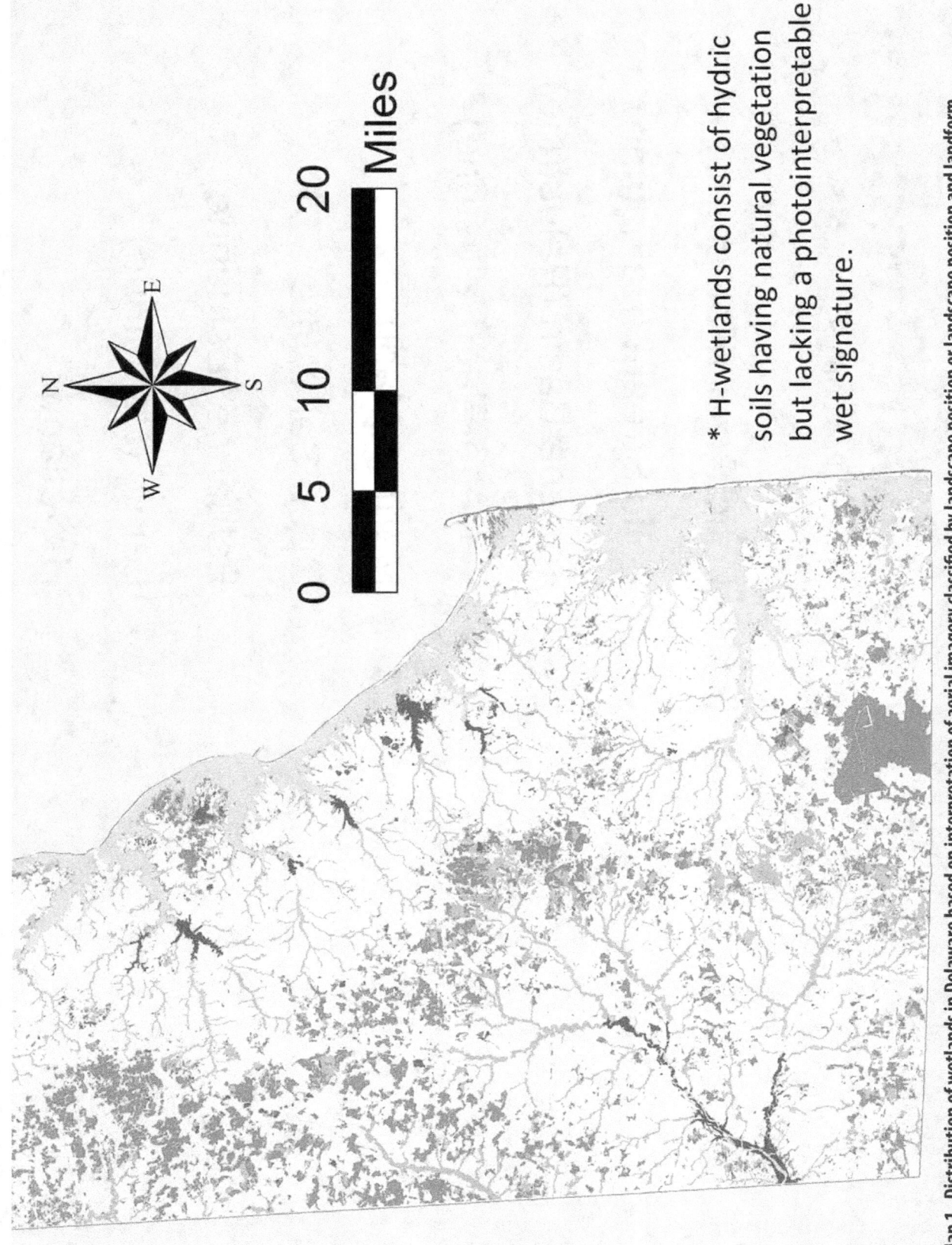

Miles

* H-wetlands consist of hydric soils having natural vegetation but lacking a photointerpretable wet signature.

Map 1. Distribution of wetlands in Delaware based on interpretation of aerial imagery classified by landscape position and landform, and ecological system. (Note: the 320,076 acres of mapped wetlands includes 62,291 of H-wetlands - hydric soil areas with natural vegetation but lacking a photointerpretable wet signature.)

Roughly half of the state's wetlands were identified in terrene landscape positions with either isolated (completely surrounded by upland) or outflow (the source of streams, or adjacent to but upgradient of other wetlands and not subject to overbank flooding) water flow paths (Table 2). These types represented nearly three-quarters (75 percent) of the palustrine wetlands. Wetlands along rivers and streams and subject to periodic overflow (lotic types) accounted for about 19 percent of the state's wetlands with most of these found along streams less than 25 feet wide. Shallow-water wetlands of ponds and impoundments (lentic) each occupied about two percent of the wetlands or three percent of the palustrine wetlands. Nearly 25 percent of the state's wetlands were associated with salt and brackish waters (24% - estuarine - with estuaries and <1% - marine - with the Atlantic Ocean).

Flat was the most common wetland landform in the state, with more than half (54%) of the state's wetlands in this landform. This was not surprising given the dominance of the coastal plain and its nearly level topography across Delaware's landscape. Fringe wetlands were the next most abundant wetland by landform, representing about one-fifth of the state's wetlands. This landform characterized the majority (81%) of the estuarine wetlands and had unobstructed connection to tidal embayments. The rest of the estuarine wetlands were either classified as island types essentially the same as fringe types but completely surrounded by water (12%) or as basin types that were located behind roads, dikes, or similar structures (7%). About 20 percent of the state's wetlands were located in distinct depressions (basin types and ponds) with the majority located in stream valleys. Floodplain wetlands associated with major rivers were rather limited, accounting for less than two percent of the wetlands.

When considering the directional flow of water, wetlands can be grouped as bidirectional flow (two-way flowage), unidirectional (throughflow, outflow, inflow), or isolated (water table rises and falls with no surface water inflow or outflow). Outflow wetlands and bidirectional-tidal wetlands were the most common water flow paths associated with Delaware wetlands (Table 2). The outflow types represented half of the state's wetlands while bidirectional wetlands accounted for more than a quarter of the wetlands. Throughflow wetlands, typically associated with nontidal rivers and streams, comprised 14 percent of the wetlands. Geographically isolated wetlands (completely surrounded by upland), which are not necessarily hydrologically isolated (when groundwater interactions are considered), represented ten percent, while bidirectional-nontidal wetlands used to characterize the hydrodynamics of large freshwater impoundments (e.g., lakes and reservoirs) accounted for less than one percent (0.24%) of the state's wetlands.

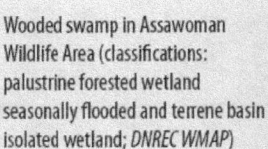

Wooded swamp in Assawoman Wildlife Area (classifications: palustrine forested wetland seasonally flooded and terrene basin isolated wetland; *DNREC WMAP*)

[3] All photointerpreted wetlands were classified by abiotic properties for use in predicting wetland functions. Farmed wetlands were excluded from this process because their functions are severely impaired by drainage and cultivation.

Table 2. 2007 acreage of wetlands classified by abiotic properties. (Note: Farmed wetlands are included at bottom but are not classified by abiotic properties.)

Landscape Position	Landform	Water Flow Path	Acreage	Landscape Position	Landform	Water Flow Path	Acreage
Marine	Fringe	Bidirectional-tidal	667	Terrene	Basin	Bidirectional-tidal	36
	Total Marine Wetlands		667			Isolated	5,807
Estuarine	Basin	Bidirectional-tidal	5,366			Outflow Intermittent	7,367
	Fringe	Bidirectional-tidal	61,814			Outflow Perennial	13,336
	Island	Bidirectional-tidal	8,815			Throughflow Intermittent	108
	Total Estuarine Wetlands		75,995			Throughflow Perennial	292
Lentic	Basin	Bidirectional-nontidal	342		Flat	Bidirectional-tidal	7
		Isolated	247			Isolated	22,220
		Throughflow Perennial	1,368			Outflow Intermittent	44,046
		Outflow Perennial	78			Outflow Perennial	92,408
	Basin	Bidirectional-nontidal	283			Throughflow Intermittent	751
	Fringe	Bidirectional-nontidal	161			Throughflow Perennial	1,526
	Island	Bidirectional-nontidal	10		Fringe	Bidirectional-tidal	6
	Total Lentic Wetlands		2,489			Isolated	69
Lotic River	Floodplain	Throughflow	498			Outflow Intermittent	14
		Bidirectional-nontidal	4,288			Outflow Perennial	59
	Fringe	Throughflow	2			Throughflow Perennial	276
		Bidirectional-nontidal	17				
	Island	Bidirectional-nontidal	6		Total Terrene Wetlands		188,328
	Total Lotic River Wetlands		4,811	Pond		Bidirectional-tidal	158
Lotic Stream	Basin	Bidirectional-tidal	1,803			Isolated	3,658
		Outflow Intermittent	48			Outflow Intermittent	409
		Throughflow Perennial	24,432			Outflow Perennial	691
		Throughflow Intermittent	2,077			Throughflow Perennial	1,103
		Bidirectional-tidal	291			Throughflow Intermittent	259
	Flat	Outflow Intermittent	114				
		Throughflow Perennial	10,089		Total Pond Wetlands		6,278
		Throughflow Intermittent	1,279				
		Bidirectional-tidal	130	Farmed Wetlands			679
	Fringe	Throughflow Perennial	547				
		Throughflow Intermittent	19	TOTAL MAPPED			320,076
	Total Lotic Stream Wetlands		40,829				

Forces Changing Wetlands

Natural processes and human actions affect wetlands in various ways. Changes in vegetation often result from natural events such as droughts, hurricanes, episodic floods, fire, and animal actions. Rising sea level also produces long-term changes in wetland hydrology and the extent of estuarine waters and wetlands. Grazing by snow geese has a tremendous impact on the vegetation of many Delaware wetlands, especially tidal wetlands where large eat-out areas have occurred exposing the area to increased erosion and subsidence.

Figure 9.

This time series of aerial photos over the west Fenwick Island area shows changes in land use between 1992 (top) and 2007 (bottom). Notice changes in forest cover (mostly forested wetlands) and increase in ponds which perform fewer wetland functions than natural wetlands. **Areas outlined in green represent only the wetlands in these areas which changed or were impacted between 1992 and 2007.**

People have had both positive and negative impacts on wetlands. Unfortunately, most human activities to date have caused wetland loss and degradation (Figure 9). For example, Delaware may have lost as much as 54 percent of its wetlands since the 1780s.[4] Human impacts to Delaware wetlands have included: 1) filling for commercial, industrial, and residential real estate, 2) disposal of dredged material and garbage (e.g., sanitary landfills), 3) dredging for navigation and marinas, 4) conversion to cropland or pasture, 5) conversion of natural wetland forests to pine plantations, 6) creation of diked impoundments for water supply and wildlife management, 7) pond construction, 8) alteration of hydrology (e.g., drainage and channelization projects), 9) direct or indirect discharge of pollutants (e.g., oil, pesticides, herbicides, and other chemicals, sediment, domestic sewage, and agricultural wastes), and 10) spreading invasive and/or exotic species (e.g., common reed and Japanese honeysuckle).

Since the 1970s, government has increased protection and management of wetlands through state and federal laws. These actions have helped to reduce human impacts, although numerous wetlands, especially hydrologically and geographically isolated wetlands, remain largely unprotected due to shortcomings in regulations and the uncertainty about which wetlands are regulated due to Supreme Court decisions. Natural resource agencies have also initiated wetland restoration programs to improve the quality of degraded wetlands and increase wetland acreage (e.g., bring back lost wetlands and create new ones). To date, over 430 existing wetland restoration projects completed by federal, State and local agencies, non-profits and private organizations, are logged into the state's restoration database and over 15,000 feet of stream channel and adjacent banks have been restored in cooperation with multiple partners.

Wetland Trends

Trends in wetland acreage differed greatly by wetland type and gross gains and losses revealed patterns that net change figures may understate (Figure 10). The greatest loss occurred to

palustrine forested wetlands (2,670 acres) while the gains were primarily ponds (2,365 acres). Comparison of only net changes would obscure the fact that ponds provide less functions and services than natural wetlands. Estuarine vegetated wetlands experienced a net loss of 21 acres. Palustrine emergent wetlands were the only natural wetland type where gains exceeded losses (net gain of 84 acres).

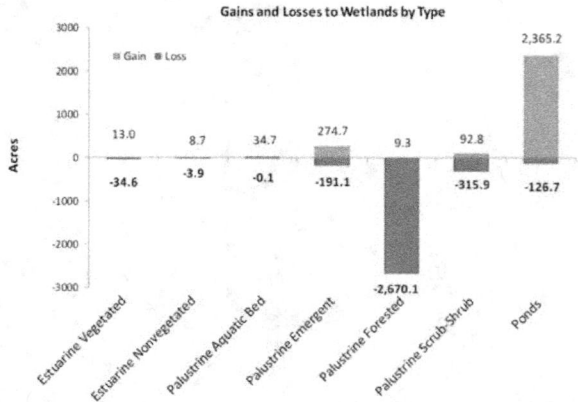

Figure 10. Gross acreage gains and losses of Delaware wetland types for 1992-2007. Does not include acreages of 'change' from one wetland type to another wetland type.

Statewide Vegetated Wetland Changes

Nearly 3,900 acres of vegetated wetlands were converted to non-wetland land uses or open water from 1992 to 2007, while only 768 acres of new vegetated wetlands were established. The latter acreage mostly consisted of estuarine marshes recently formed in shallow water and palustrine emergent wetlands established on farmland that was not cultivated in 2007 (Table 3, Map 2). These changes resulted in a net loss of 3,126 acres of vegetated wetlands.

Including changes to wetland type, estuarine vegetated wetlands experienced a net loss of 238 acres from 1992 to 2007 (Table 3). Most of the 580 acres of gross loss resulted from the submergence of marshes: either conversion to open water (482 acres) or to nonvegetated intertidal wetlands (56 acres; Figure 11).

[4]Dahl, T.E. 1990. Wetland Losses in the United States, 1780s to 1980s. U.S. Department of Interior, Fish and Wildlife Service, Washington, DC. Report to Congress.

Smaller losses were due to residential, commercial and highway development (22 acres), conversion to natural sandy areas (13 acres), and pond construction (7 acres). Gross gains in estuarine emergent wetlands (341 acres) came mostly from conversion of estuarine open water (328 acres) as well as smaller gains from agricultural land, transitional land and altered/barren land (Table 3).

Palustrine vegetated wetlands experienced a <u>net</u> loss of nearly 2,900 acres between 1992 and 2007, with 3,314 acres of losses and 426 acres of gains recorded (Table 3). The main causes for the 3,314-acre gross palustrine vegetated wetland loss was to agricultural activities (1,082 acres) and residential development (861 acres) which together accounted for nearly 60 percent of the losses (Figure 12). Clearing to create "altered/barren land" that may be under development together with "transitional land" that is under construction (943 acres) accounted for another 28 percent of gross loss. Other forms of development in wetlands, excavation of wetlands for pond and lake construction, highway and road construction through wetlands, creation of recreational land,

Sources of Palustrine Vegetated Wetland Losses

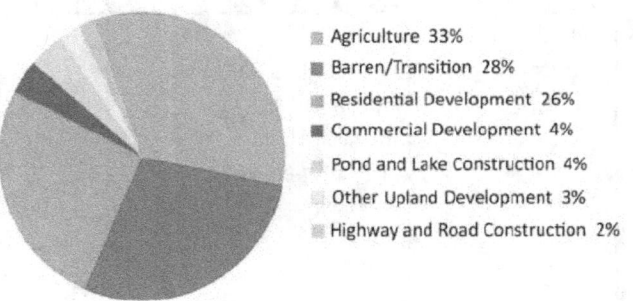

- Agriculture 33%
- Barren/Transition 28%
- Residential Development 26%
- Commercial Development 4%
- Pond and Lake Construction 4%
- Other Upland Development 3%
- Highway and Road Construction 2%

Figure 12. Proportion of gross palustrine vegetated wetland loss by source.

and farmed wetlands made up the remaining 13 percent of gross wetland loss. Over 400 acres of gross gains occurred, mostly from the conversion of agricultural land (169 acres) and altered/barren land (181 acres).

By ecological class, forested wetlands were the most heavily impacted of the palustrine vegetated wetlands with a <u>net</u> loss of 2,931 acres (9 acres of gains and 2,940 acres of losses). Scrub-shrub wetlands had a <u>net</u> loss of 213 acres, while emergent wetlands increased by 207 acres. Timber harvest of forested wetlands contributed 139 acres to the gain in emergent wetlands and also created 21 acres of scrub-shrub wetlands. This timbered acreage should revert to forested wetlands over time, if not converted to another land use. Some shifts in other vegetation types were also detected. Hydrology changes, possibly attributed to sea-level rise, coastal subsidence, or other factors, transformed 287 acres of estuarine emergent wetlands to aquatic beds. These vegetation type changes had little effect on overall gains or losses in vegetated wetlands, although they resulted in changes in some functions.

Sources of Estuarine Wetland Losses

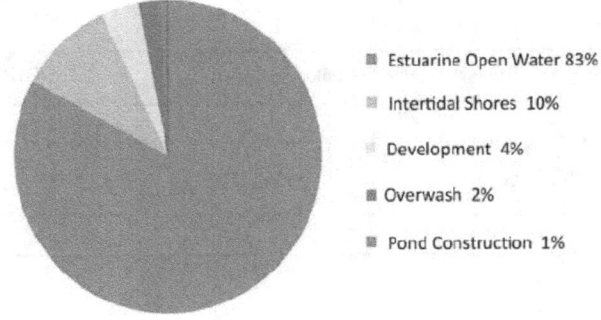

- Estuarine Open Water 83%
- Intertidal Shores 10%
- Development 4%
- Overwash 2%
- Pond Construction 1%

Figure 11. Proportion of gross estuarine vegetated wetland loss by source.

Table 3. Statewide changes in vegetated wetlands: 1992-2007. Acreages reflect gains, losses and changes.

Wetland Change	Source	Acreage Affected
Estuarine Vegetated Gain from	Estuarine Open Water	328.2
	Agricultural Land	6.9
	Transitional Land	4.8
	Altered/Barren Land	1.3
	Total Gain	+341.2
Estuarine Vegetated Loss to	Estuarine Open Water	481.9
	Intertidal Unconsolidated Shore	56.0
	Residential Development	14.4
	Natural Sandy Area	13.2
	Pond Construction	6.9
	Commercial Development	6.7
	Highway/Road	0.4
	Total Loss	-579.5
	Net Estuarine Vegetated Wetland Change =	-238.3 (Loss)

Wetland Change	Source	Acreage Affected
Palustrine Vegetated Gain from	Agricultural Land	169.1
	Altered/Barren Land	180.6
	Pond Colonization	15.0
	Upland Forest	14.5
	Pasture	12.4
	Transitional Land	11.2
	Industrial Land	8.9
	Farmed Wetland	6.7
	Residential Land	3.2
	Commercial Land	3.2
	Rangeland	1.1
	Natural Sandy Area	0.4
	Total Gain	+426.3
Palustrine Vegetated Loss to	Agriculture	1,082.0
	Residential Development	860.6
	Altered/Barren Land	594.9
	Transitional Land	348.0
	Commercial Development	127.8
	Pond Construction	93.0
	Highway/Road Construction	65.3
	Golf Course Construction	45.9
	Lake Construction	42.4
	Other Recreational Land	33.5
	Unknown	12.4
	Industrial Development	2.8
	Estuarine Water	4.4
	Railroad Construction	0.6
	Farmed Wetland	0.3
	Total Loss	-3,313.9
	Net Palustrine Vegetated Wetland Change =	- 2,887.6 (Loss)
	TOTAL Net Change in Vegetated Wetland =	-3,125.9 (Loss)

STATEWIDE NONVEGETATED WETLAND CHANGES

Pond acreage increased statewide by 2,285 acres between 1992 and 2007, with 2,430 acres of new ponds created, and a 145-acre loss of pre-existing ponds (Table 4). Nonvegetated wetland ponds are technically considered wetlands, but the artificial ones typically do not provide functions equivalent to natural wetlands. Approximately two-thirds (65%) of the gross pond acreage gain was built on former agricultural land for stormwater purposes associated with new residential and commercial development (Figure 13). Overall, 93 percent of the new ponds were constructed in uplands, whereas only seven percent came from wetlands (mostly from forested wetlands and farmed wetlands; Table 4). Ponds were mostly filled by altered/barren land (19%), agricultural uses (18%) and the creation of transitional land (18%). In addition to pond changes, 180 acres of shallow-water lacustrine wetlands (borrow pits) were created from uplands (151.4 acres) and from vegetated wetlands (28.7 acres).

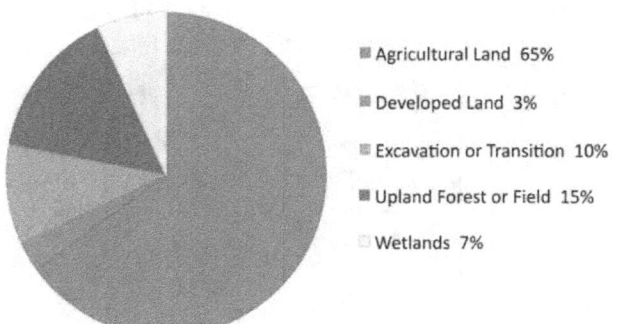

Sources of Gains in Ponds

- Agricultural Land 65%
- Developed Land 3%
- Excavation or Transition 10%
- Upland Forest or Field 15%
- Wetlands 7%

Figure 13. Causes for gains in nonvegetated wetland ponds in Delaware 1992-2007.

Estuarine tidal flats experienced a <u>net</u> loss of 10 acres. Interestingly, 81 acres of new tidal flats were established: 56 acres in former salt marshes (36.4 acres in emergent and 19.5 acres in scrub-shrub wetlands), 24 acres in former estuarine open water, and less than two acres in former residential land. However, about 87 acres of pre-existing flats were converted to estuarine open water (86.7) and a pond (0.6 acres), while four acres were filled for commercial land.

The increase in stormwater ponds, while important for surface water detention, are no substitute for the multitude of functions provided by natural wetlands (classifications: palustrine unconsolidated bottom wetland semipermanently flooded and terrene pond isolated wetland; *Rebecca Rothweiler, DNREC WMAP*)

Table 4. Estimated changes in ponds in Delaware: 1992-2007.

Nature of Change	Source	Acreage
Gain	Agricultural Land	1,565.9 (includes 122.0 from pasture)
	Upland Forest	271.6
	Altered/Barren Land	128.1
	Transitional Land	118.2
	Rangeland	99.1
	Palustrine Forested Wetland	75.1
	Farmed Wetland	70.8
	Industrial Land	28.4
	Residential Land	24.4
	Commercial Land	15.2
	Palustrine Scrub-Shrub Wetland	13.3
	Estuarine Wetland	7.5
	Palustrine Emergent Wetland	4.0
	Golf Course	3.7
	Confined Feeding Operations	3.5
	Mixed Commercial/Industrial Land	0.6
	Sand/Gravel Pits	0.6
	Other Recreational Land	0.1
	Total Gain	**+2,430.1**
Loss	Altered/Barren Land	27.9
	Agricultural Land	26.6
	Transitional Land	26.1
	Commercial Development	16.9
	Residential Development	14.7
	Palustrine Emergent Wetland	10.7
	Industrial Development	6.2
	Palustrine Scrub-Shrub Wetland	4.4
	Highway/Road	3.7
	Lacustrine Deepwater	3.5
	Golf Course	2.1
	Sand/Gravel Pits	1.5
	Rangeland	0.8
	Other Recreational Land	0.1
	Total Loss	**-145.2**
Net Change	=	+2,284.9(Gain)

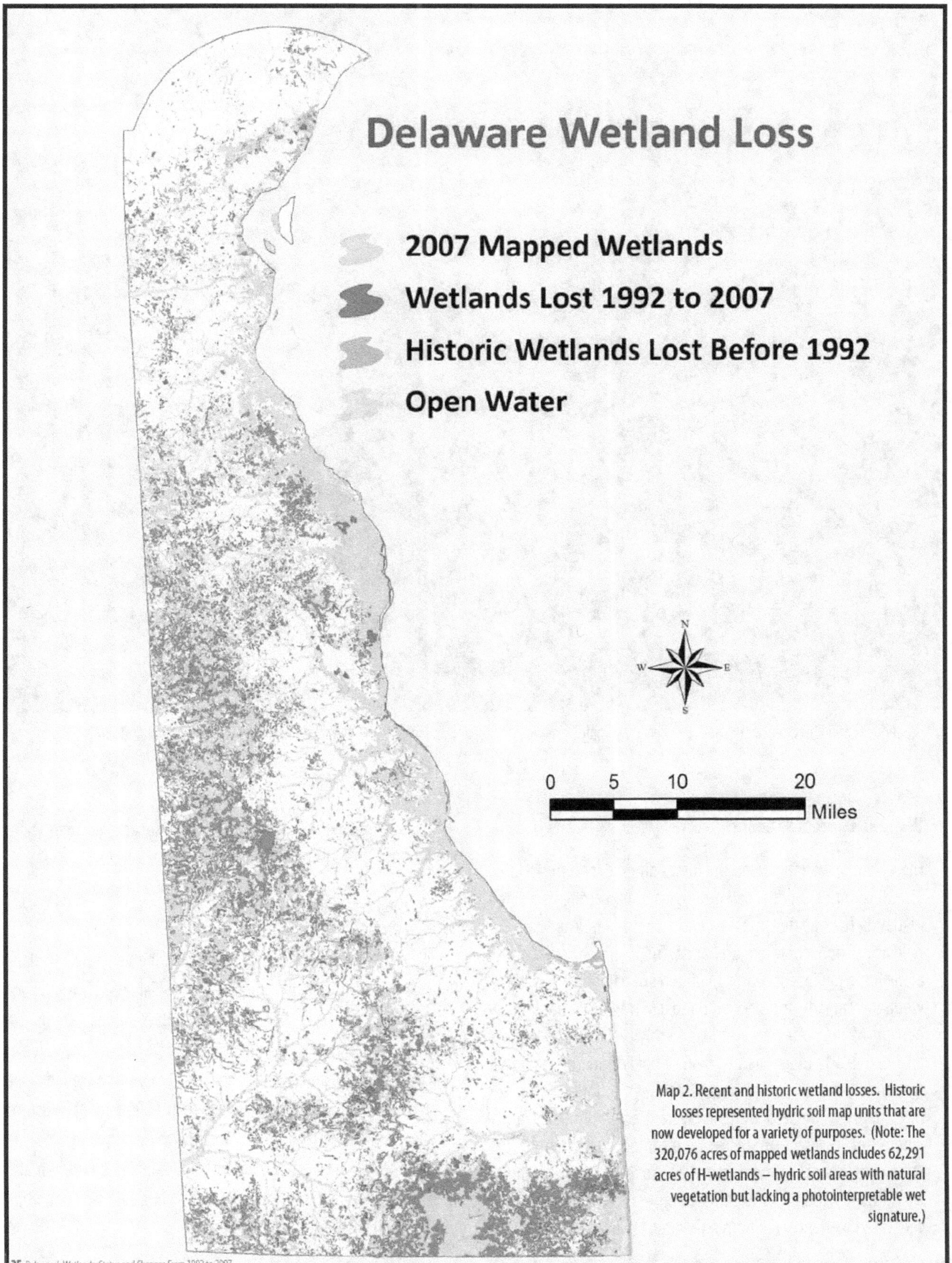

Delaware Wetland Loss

- 2007 Mapped Wetlands
- Wetlands Lost 1992 to 2007
- Historic Wetlands Lost Before 1992
- Open Water

0   5   10   20
Miles

Map 2. Recent and historic wetland losses. Historic losses represented hydric soil map units that are now developed for a variety of purposes. (Note: The 320,076 acres of mapped wetlands includes 62,291 acres of H-wetlands – hydric soil areas with natural vegetation but lacking a photointerpretable wet signature.)

Wetland in Blackbird Creek watershed (classifications: palustrine forested wetland seasonally flooded and terrene basin isolated wetland; *DNREC WMAP*)

WETLAND CHANGES BY COUNTY

The extent of wetland gains and losses differed by county (Table 5). All counties experienced net losses of palustrine vegetated wetlands (freshwater marshes and swamps) and net gains of palustrine nonvegetated wetlands (ponds). Sussex County alone had a net loss of nearly 2,600 acres of palustrine vegetated wetlands (mostly forested wetlands). This amounted to 89 percent of the statewide net loss of this type. Sussex County also had nearly twice the net gain of palustrine nonvegetated wetlands (mostly created ponds) as other counties. Changes of estuarine vegetated wetlands were greatest in Kent County where net losses of 165 acres represented 69 percent of the statewide loss of this type from 1992 to 2007. Sussex County was the only county to experience a net increase in estuarine vegetated wetlands – a nominal gain of two acres. Both Kent

and Sussex Counties gained acreage in lacustrine open water wetlands through construction of borrow pits.

WETLAND CHANGES BY BASIN

All basins recorded a net loss of palustrine vegetated wetland acreage and a net gain in pond acreage (Table 5). Two drainage basins - Chesapeake Bay and Inland Bays Basins - each lost over 1,000 acres of palustrine vegetated wetlands. These losses accounted for 96 percent of the state's net loss of this wetland type. The Delaware Bay Basin gained more than 1,000 acres of palustrine nonvegetated wetlands which represented nearly half (46%) of the statewide net increase in ponds. The Inland Bays Basin also experienced a large increase in ponds (644 acres), accounting for 28 percent of the statewide change.

Table 5. Wetland losses and gains in Delaware's counties and drainage basins: 1992-2007. Note: Sums may differ slightly from state totals due to round-off procedures.

Geographic Area	Wetland Type	Gain	Loss	Net Change
New Castle County	Estuarine Vegetated	5.5	80.3	-74.8
	Estuarine Nonvegetated	0.0	25.5	-25.5
	Palustrine Vegetated	166.4	208.6	-42.2
	Palustrine Nonvegetated	665.7	39.5	+626.2
Kent County	Estuarine Vegetated	322.1	487.2	-165.1
	Estuarine Nonvegetated	57.0	64.3	-7.3
	Palustrine Vegetated	187.6	451.7	-264.1
	Palustrine Nonvegetated	625.3	42.7	+582.6
	Lacustrine Nonvegetated	129.3	0.0	+129.3
Sussex County	Marine Nonvegetated	0.7	0.0	+0.7
	Estuarine Vegetated	13.6	11.6	+2.0
	Estuarine Nonvegetated	24.3	1.4	+22.9
	Palustrine Vegetated	72.5	2,656.3	-2,583.8
	Palustrine Nonvegetated	1,138.0	64.9	+1,073.4
	Lacustrine Nonvegetated	50.8	0.0	+50.8
Delaware Bay Drainage Basin	Estuarine Vegetated	327.6	545.4	-217.8
	Estuarine Nonvegetated	58.3	86.7	-28.4
	Palustrine Vegetated	244.2	401.8	-157.6
	Palustrine Nonvegetated	1,108.6	58.1	+1,050.5
	Lacustrine Nonvegetated	129.3	0.0	+129.3
Chesapeake Bay Drainage Basin	Palustrine Vegetated	47.1	1,814.7	-1,767.6
	Palustrine Nonvegetated	471.5	29.8	+441.7
	Lacustrine Nonvegetated	50.8	0.0	+50.8
Inland Bays/Atlantic Ocean Basin	Marine Nonvegetated	0.7	0.0	+0.7
	Estuarine Vegetated	13.6	9.3	+4.3
	Estuarine Nonvegetated	23.8	0.0	+23.8
	Palustrine Vegetated	33.0	1,045.9	-1,012.9
	Palustrine Nonvegetated	675.6	31.3	+644.3
Piedmont	Estuarine Vegetated	0.0	24.6	-24.6
	Estuarine Nonvegetated	0.0	4.5	-4.5
	Palustrine Vegetated	102.2	54.5	+47.7
	Palustrine Nonvegetated	174.1	22.7	+151.4

Significance of Recent Wetland Changes on Wetland Functions

Wetland scientists recognize that all wetlands do not necessarily provide all wetland functions at the same level of performance. Features like vegetation type, hydrology, landscape position, landform, and connectivity (linkage to other wetlands and waters) provide individual wetlands with certain opportunities to perform different functions. While reporting on acreage of wetland losses and gains gives us perspective on the extent of the changes relative to existing resources, these acreage differences say little about the effect of those changes on wetland functions. The expanded abiotic classification employed for the current inventory was used to make predictions about the potential of wetlands to perform eleven functions during the reporting period (Table 6). The following functions were predicted:

Functions predicted:	
Surface water detention	Coastal storm surge detention
Streamflow maintenance	Nutrient transformation
Carbon sequestration	Sediment and other particulates retention
Bank and shoreline stabilization	Provision of habitat for other wildlife
Provision of waterfowl and waterbird habitat	Provision of fish and aquatic invertebrate habitat
Provision of unique, uncommon or highly diverse wetland plant communities	

It is important to emphasize that this assessment focuses on the potential of wetlands to perform functions at the landscape-scale based on NWIPlus classifications of wetlands and functional correlations developed for the Northeast (Tiner 2003b with recent revisions). Field assessment is required to determine the actual level of functional performance for a wetland as alterations to natural wetlands affect their ability to fully perform one or multiple functions. Additionally, this assessment of function does not examine wetland condition or quality but rather the potential for certain types of wetlands to perform different functions. For information on wetland condition, readers should refer to DNREC's watershed reports on wetland condition listed in the Wetland Resource Guide at the end of this booklet. These field-based investigations consider ecological quality and the impacts of adjacent land use in evaluating wetland condition.

The current landscape analysis suggested that the following functions are potentially being performed at high or moderate levels by at least two-thirds of the state's wetlands: *surface water detention, nutrient transformation, carbon sequestration, bank and shoreline stabilization, and provision of habitat for other wildlife* (Table 6). Other functions potentially provided at high or moderate levels by more than 40 percent of the state's wetlands are: *streamflow maintenance, sediment and other particulates retention, and provision of habitat for waterfowl, waterbirds, fish and aquatic invertebrates*. One-third of Delaware's wetlands are important for *coastal storm surge detention*, and roughly one-fifth serve as vital *habitat for unique, uncommon, or highly diverse plant communities*.

Table 6. Acreage of 2007 wetlands (including ponds) predicted to perform each wetland function at high or moderate levels, percent of the state's 2007 wetlands that they represent, and the wetland acreage of gain (+) or loss (-) from 1992-2007. Farmed wetlands and areas mapped as H-wetlands were not included in this assessment or in the state total for determining the percentages.

Wetland Function	2007 Acreage	% of DE's Wetlands likely performing at moderate to high levels in 2007	Acreage Change 1992 to 2007
1. Surface Water Detention (This function is limited to freshwater wetlands; the role of coastal wetlands in water storage is handled by the Coastal Storm Surge Detention function.)	171,045	66.5	-414
2. Coastal Storm Surge Detention (This function includes tidal wetlands plus contiguous nontidal wetlands subject to flooding during storm surges.)	83,523	32.5	-180
3. Streamflow Maintenance (These wetlands are sources of streams or along first order perennial streams or above.)	134,620	52.4	-5,888
4. Nutrient Transformation	246,847	96.0	-3,422
5. Carbon Sequestration	249,012	96.9	-3,162
6. Sediment and Other Particulates Retention	156,756	61.0	-2,141
7. Bank and Shoreline Stabilization	182,105	70.7	-1,383
8. Fish and Aquatic Invertebrate Habitat Stream Shading	78,230 36,935	30.5 14.4	+123 -31
9. Waterfowl and Waterbird Habitat Wood Duck	80,920 25,691	31.5 10.0	+104 +147
10. Other Wildlife Habitat	248,090	96.5	-3,119
11. Unique, Uncommon, or Highly Diverse Wetland Plant Communities (The following types are included in this category: estuarine aquatic beds, regularly flooded salt marsh (low marsh), slightly brackish tidal marshes, tidal freshwater flats (e.g., wild rice beds), marshes and shrub swamps, Atlantic white cedar swamps, bald cypress swamps, and lotic fringe wetlands.)	54,963	21.4	-372

Changes in Delaware's wetlands between 1992 and 2007 have increased some types (mainly ponds) and decreased vegetated types, which causes changes in the functions that are associated with these wetland types. By adding ponds to the landscape which were previously upland, the functional potential of the state's wetlands increased slightly for a few functions, namely provision of fish and invertebrate habitat, and provision of habitat for waterfowl and waterbirds. These created wetlands do not compensate for the heavy losses of vegetated wetlands in natural settings that provide a wide range of functions. Functions that experienced significant declines due to losses of wetlands from 1992-2007 were streamflow maintenance, provision of other wildlife habitat, nutrient transformation, carbon sequestration, sediment retention, and bank and shoreline stabilization.

Future of Delaware Wetlands

Although there is increased interest and study of wetlands today, and more wetland conservation and management performed by agencies and organizations, loss of wetland area and function continues. The previous trends report for the period 1981/2-1992 estimated a statewide net loss of 1,906 acres of vegetated wetlands, or 190 acres annually. The findings from the current study for the period of 1992-2007 reported a net loss of 3,126 acres of vegetated wetlands, or 208 acres annually. This represents a nine percent increase in annual loss. Not only is Delaware losing wetland acreage, but the wetlands that remain are being impacted through secondary effects (e.g., adjacent development, fragmentation, and water quality degradation) that diminish the functions and services they provide. For example, completed watershed-wide wetland condition assessments show that the majority of wetlands in the Nanticoke, Inland Bays, and St. Jones River watersheds are degraded to some extent and only a small portion of the remaining wetlands are functioning similar to reference (minimally disturbed) wetlands. Primary stressors include alterations to the hydrology (e.g., ditching and channelization), to the vegetation community (e.g., timber harvest and invasive species), and lack of naturally vegetated buffers to protect wetlands from disturbance by surrounding land use activities (for more information see http://www.dnrec.delaware.gov/wr/Information/OtherInfo/Pages/WetlandMonitoringandAssessment.aspx). The gains in wetland acreage during the 1992-2007 time period show that the majority of gains are constructed ponds, typically borrow pits, stormwater, and irrigation ponds which provide less functions than natural wetlands.

Nontidal wetlands in Delaware are regulated under Section 404 and 401 of the Clean Water Act by the U.S. Army Corps of Engineers. Efforts by the Corps in the 1980s and early 1990s helped significantly reduce wetland impacts. In 1989, the federal government adopted a goal of no-net-loss for the regulatory program. Although this goal has helped improve the awareness of wetlands values, the results in this report show that no-net loss has not been achieved in Delaware. Given the development boom beginning in the mid-1990s and recent court decisions, wetland protection seemed to be moving away from improvements made in the early 1990s. Changes in federal regulations stemming from Supreme Court decisions (i.e., Solid Waste Agency of Northern Cook County, Rapanos, and Carabell cases) have left the jurisdiction over many isolated wetlands, including Delmarva bays, coastal plain ponds, and headwater flatwoods, uncertain. Site-by-site reviews are now made by the Corps to determine federal jurisdiction.

Since 1973, the State of Delaware has been regulating activities in tidal wetlands under the "Wetlands Act" which requires any work within tidal wetlands, if approved, to receive a permit from the state. This program has been effective at managing human impacts to tidal wetlands but today's threats to tidal wetlands appear to be driven by larger forces beyond the scope of any wetland regulatory program (e.g., sea-level rise and coastal submergence) and not by site-specific impacts. Tidal wetland acreage loss has slightly increased recently. Although there was a gain (341 acres) in tidal wetlands due to restoration and natural processes during these 15 years, the losses (579 acres) were greater. The net loss of tidal wetlands from all causes equates to almost 16 acres per year versus a 10-acre annual loss rate from 1981/2-1992. The dominant cause from 1981/2-1992 interval was human-induced land use changes. Now the major cause of tidal marsh loss, the conversion of tidal wetlands to open water, is likely due to rising sea level attributed to climate change. Additional studies are underway in Delaware to better understand these impacts on tidal wetlands.

In an effort to improve wetland regulation and management in Delaware, DNREC contracted an outside source to conduct an independent review of Delaware's statewide wetland programs and provide constructive feedback and recommendations. The Environmental Law Institute (ELI) used previous research, literature review and extensive interview results to produce a review of the state's regulatory and non-regulatory wetlands programs, a list of major challenges facing wetland protection in the state, and narratives of opportunities to improve wetland protection through existing programs or regulations and through additional programs or regulations. The full report by ELI can be found on the Delaware Wetlands website (http://www.dnrec.delaware.gov/Admin/DelawareWetlands) under Restoration and Protection.

Wetland conservation and restoration efforts continue to grow in Delaware. The DNREC recognizes the importance of ecological restoration, which targets both wetland and stream restoration projects. There has been improved coordination between agencies such as DNREC, the U.S. Fish and Wildlife Service, the U.S.D.A. Natural Resource Conservation Service, county conservation districts, and private conservation partners to leverage funding to accomplish more and higher quality restoration. Watershed restoration strategies continue to be developed to prioritize project type and location based on documented impacts and needs at the watershed level. These plans focus resources to gain the greatest benefit for improving and sustaining our natural resources for the future. Restoration priorities are usually multi-faceted including land conservation (both upland and wetland set-aside), wetland and stream restoration, reconnection of floodplains, planting buffers, and invasive species management.

Although wetland restoration and conservation efforts have improved, the forces changing the landscape of Delaware remain as significant threats to wetlands. During the 15 years of this study, a real estate boom led to a major increase in residential and commercial development and associated infrastructure. This growth produced more and wider roads (expanding impervious surface), increased the need for drainage, raised demand for good fill dirt from extraction/borrow pits, and accelerated construction of stormwater detention ponds. Secondary effects from this growth also degraded existing wetlands and reduced their functions. Many of the impacts are focused on headwater palustrine forests which are among the state's most important wetlands for flood control and water quality. The costs associated with trying to replace these lost or diminished functions often are much higher than the costs of preserving these wetlands.

Wetlands are the vital link between land and water – a critical resource for all Delawareans. Work is still needed to better protect wetland habitats and their functions, and wherever possible, to restore wetlands, streams, and their buffers. These goals require cooperation and compromise between government, the business community, and private landowners. By working together, Delawareans will continue to reap the benefits from the state's wetland resources that help protect property, human health and safety, and contribute to a high quality of life today and for future generations, while providing vital habitat for native plants, and resident and migratory animals.

While admiring the
expanse and beauty
of one of
Delaware's wetlands,
what will she see
when she takes
her grandchildren on
the same walk in
sixty years?
(*Autumn Schneider*)

Wetland Contacts

For additional information on wetlands contact the following agencies:

The Delaware Department of Natural Resources and Environmental Control's Delaware Wetlands website is a comprehensive location for information on Delaware's conservation partners, wetland regulations, wetland restoration and protection, wetland mapping and data resources, wetland types, ecosystem services, education, monitoring and assessment, status and trends, and the Delaware Wetlands Conservation Strategy.
http://www.dnrec.delaware.gov/Admin/DelawareWetlands

Delaware Department of Natural Resources and Environmental Control
Wetlands and Subaqueous Lands Section
89 Kings Highway
Dover, DE 19901
302-739-9943
http://www.wr.dnrec.delaware.gov/Services/Pages/WetlandsAndSubaqueousLands.aspx

U.S. Fish and Wildlife Service
Ecological Services (NWI)
300 Westgate Center Drive
Hadley, MA 01035
413-253-8620
http://www.fws.gov/northeast/wetlands/

U.S. Fish and Wildlife Service
Delaware Bay Estuary Project
2610 Whitehall Neck Road
Smyrna, DE 19977
302-653-9152
http://www.fws.gov/delawarebay/index.html

EPA Wetland Protection Hotline
1-800-832-7828
http://www.epa.gov/OWOW/wetlands/wetline.html

U.S. Army Corps of Engineers
Philadelphia District
Regulatory Branch
100 Penn Square East
Wanamaker Building
Philadelphia, PA 19107
215-656-6728
http://www.usace.army.mil/CECW/Pages/cecwo_reg.aspx

U.S. Army Corps of Engineers
Dover Field Office
1203 College Park Drive
Suite 103
Dover, DE 19904
302-736-9763

Wetland Resource Guide (includes reports referenced in the text)

To learn more about wetlands, review the following readings:

Classification of Wetlands and Deepwater Habitats of the United States (1979) by L.M. Cowardin, V. Carter, F.C. Golet, and E.T. LaRoe, U.S. Fish and Wildlife Service, Washington, DC. http://wetlands.fws.gov

Condition of Nontidal Wetlands in the Nanticoke River Watershed, Maryland and Delaware (2008) by A.D. Jacobs and D.F. Bleil. Delaware Department of Natural Resources and Environmental Control, Watershed Assessment Section, Dover, DE 19904; 302-739-9939.

Correlating Enhanced National Wetlands Inventory Data with Wetland Functions for Watershed Assessments: A Rationale for Northeastern U.S. Wetlands (2003b) by R.W. Tiner. U.S. Fish and Wildlife Service, National Wetlands Inventory Program, Northeast Region, Hadley, MA. http://library.fws.gov/Wetlands/corelate_wetlandsNE.pdf

Delaware's Wetlands: Status and Recent Trends (2001) by R.W. Tiner. U.S. Fish and Wildlife Service, Northeast Region, Hadley, MA. Prepared for the DNREC, Dover, DE. http://www.fws.gov/wetlands/_documents/gSandT/StateRegionalReports/DelawaresWetlandsStatusRecentTrends.pdf

Dichotomous Keys and Mapping Codes for Wetland Landscape Position, Landform, Water Flow Path, and Waterbody Type Descriptors (2003) by R.W. Tiner. U.S. Fish and Wildlife Service, National Wetlands Inventory Program, Northeast Region, Hadley, MA. http://library.fws.gov/Wetlands/dichotomouskeys0903.pdf

Field Guide to Nontidal Wetland Identification (1988) by R. Tiner, reprinted by the Institute for Wetland & Environmental Education & Research, P.O. Box 288, Leverett, MA 01054; 413-548-8866. (guidebook for identifying wetland plants and hydric soil; Mid-Atlantic focus)

Field Guide to Tidal Wetland Plants of the Northeastern United States and Neighboring Canada (2009) by R. Tiner, University of Massachusetts Press, P.O. Box 429, Amherst, MA 01004; 413-545-2219. (technical guide to tidal wetland plant identification)

Field Indicators of Hydric Soils in the United States (2010) by L.M. Vasilas, G.W. Hurt, and C.V. Noble (eds.). U.S.D.A. Natural Resources Conservation Service in cooperation with the National Technical Committee for Hydric Soils. Available from landcare@usda.gov; 1-888-LANDCARE (526-3227). ftp://ftp-fc.sc.egov.usda.gov/NSSC/Hydric_Soils/FieldIndicators_v7.pdf (technical guide for identifying hydric soils)

Handbook for Wetlands Conservation and Sustainability (1998) by K. Firehock, L. Graff, J. Middleton, K. Starinchak, and C. Williams, Save Our Streams Program, Izaak Walton League of America, 707 Conservation Lane, Gaithersburg, MD 20878-2983; 800-BUG-IWLA. (citizen's guide to protecting, restoring, and monitoring wetlands)

In Search of Swampland: A Wetland Sourcebook and Field Guide Second Edition (2005) by R. Tiner, Rutgers University Press, P.O. Box 5062, New Brunswick, NJ 08903: 732-445-1970. (layperson's guide to wetland ecology and identification of wetland plants, soils, and animals; Northeast focus)

"NWIPlus: Geospatial database for watershed-level functional assessment" (2010) by R.W. Tiner, Environmental Law Institute, National Wetlands Newsletter 32(3): 4-7, 23. http://www.fws.gov/northeast/wetlands/Publications%20PDFs%20as%20of%20March_2008/Mapping/NWIPlus_NWN.pdf

Methods Used to Create Datasets for the Delaware State Wetlands Update (2011) by K. McGuckin, Conservation Management Institute, Virginia Polytechnic Institute and State University, Blacksburg, VA.

Our National Wetland Heritage: A Protection Guide (1996) by J. Kusler and T. Opheim, Environmental Law Institute, 1616 P Street NW, Suite 200, Washington, DC 20036; 202-939-3800. (guide to wetland protection strategies for local governments)

Statewide Wetlands Mapping Project - the SWMP (1994) by L.T. Pomatto, Jr., Delaware Department of Natural Resources and Environmental Control, Division of Water Resources, 89 Kings Highway, Dover, DE 19901. (technical report on state wetland mapping)

Wetland Condition of the Inland Bays Watershed, Volume 1: Nontidal Wetlands (2009) by A. Jacobs, A. Rogerson, D. Fillis, and C. Bason, Delaware Department of Natural Resources and Environmental Control, Watershed Assessment Section, Dover, DE 19904; 302-739-9939.

Wetlands Condition of the Inland Bays Watershed, Volume 2: Tidal Wetlands (2009) by A. Rogerson, A. Howard, and A. Jacobs, Delaware Department of Natural Resources and Environmental Control, Watershed Assessment Section, Dover, DE 19904; 302-739-9939.

Wetland Condition of the St. Jones River Watershed (2010) by A.B. Rogerson, A.D. Jacobs, and A.M. Howard, Delaware Department of Natural Resources and Environmental Control, Watershed Assessment Section, Dover, DE 19904; 302-739-9939.

Wetland Indicators: A Guide to Wetland Identification, Delineation, Classification, and Mapping (1999) by R. Tiner, Lewis Publishers, CRC Press, 2000 Corporate Boulevard NW, Boca Raton, FL 33231; 561-994-0555. (textbook with in depth review of listed topics)

Wetlands (1994) by W. Niering, National Audubon Society Nature Guide, Alfred A. Knopf, Inc., New York, NY. (introduction to wetlands and field guide to plants and animals; national focus)

Wetlands (2007) by W. Mitsch and J. Gosselink, John Wiley and Sons, Inc., New York, NY. (textbook on wetland ecology)

Wetlands: Characteristics and Boundaries (1995) by Committee on Characterization of Wetlands, National Academy Press, 2102 Constitution Avenue NW, Washington, DC 20418; 800-624-6242. (reference book on wetland delineation and related topics)

Wetlands of Delaware (1985) by R. Tiner, USFWS-NWI for Delaware Department of Natural Resources and Environmental Control, Wetlands Section, 89 Kings Highway, Dover, DE 19901; 302-739-9943. http://www.fws.gov/wetlands/_documents/g0ther/WetlandsOfDelaware.pdf (summary of wetlands information for the state)

Winter Guide to Woody Plants of Wetlands and Their Borders: Northeastern United States (1997) by R. Tiner, Institute for Wetland & Environmental Education & Research, P.O. Box 288, Leverett, MA 01054; 413-548-8866. (guidebook to winter plant identification)

Wetlands Mapping Standard (2009) by Federal Geographic Data Committee Wetlands Subcommittee, Reston, VA 22092. FGDC-STD-015-2009. http://www.fgdc.gov/standards/projects/FGDC-standards-projects/wetlands-mapping/2009-08%20FGDC%20Wetlands%20Mapping%20Standard_final.pdf

Notes: